Incredible Insects

John Townsend

Chicago, Illinois

For information, address the publisher:
Raintree, 100 N. LaSalle, Suite 1200, Chicago, IL 60602
Customer Service: 888-363-4266
Visit our website at www.raintreelibrary.com

Printed and bound in China by South China Printing Company.
09 08 07 06 05
10 9 8 7 6 5 4 3 2 1

Library of Congress Cataloging-in-Publication Data
Townsend, John, 1955-
  Incredible insects / John Townsend.
      p. cm. -- (Incredible creatures)
Summary: Introduces a variety of unusual facts about the physical characteristics and behavior of insects.
Includes bibliographical references (p.   ) and index.
  ISBN 1-4109-0530-6 (library binding : hardcover) -- ISBN 1-4109-0854-2 (pbk.)
  1. Insects--Juvenile literature. [1. Insects.] I. Title. II. Series:
Townsend, John, 1955-   Incredible creatures.
  QL467.2.T69 2005
  595.7--dc22
                          2003020103

Acknowledgments
The publishers would like to thank the following for permission to reproduce photographs: p. 4 Nature Photo Library/Bruce Davidson; p. 5 (left) RSPCA Photolibrary; pp. 5 (top, middle, bottom), 7 (left), 8, 10, 12 (left), 13, 14,16, 17, 22, 22–23, 24 (right), 26–27, 28–29, 32–33, 35, 36, 36—37, 37, 39 (left, right), 40–41 FLPA; pp. 6, 19 (top), 23 Galen Rowell/Corbis; p. 7 (right) Brian Rogers/Natural Visions; pp. 8–9, 12 (right), 15 (left, right), 16–17, 18, 19 (bottom), 25, 30, 30–31, 33, 34, 38, 40, 41, 42–43, 43, 45, 46, 46–47, 47, 48, 49 NHPA; p. 9 Andrew Cooper/Nature Picture Library; p. 11 (left) Getty Images/Stone; p. 11 (right), 29, 42, 48–49 Oxford Scientific Films; p. 20 (top) Darwin Dale/Science Photo Library; pp. 20 (bottom), 21, 27, 28 Dr. Jeremy Burgess/Science Photo Library; p. 24 (left) Bohemian Nomad Picturemakers/Corbis; p. 26 Jean Preston-Mafham/Premaphotos Wildlife; p. 32 Ken Preston Mafham/Premaphotos Wildlife; pp. 31, 44–45 Darwin Dale/Agstock/Science Photo Library; pp. 34–35 George D. Lepp/Corbis; p. 44 Premaphotos/Nature Photo Library; pp. 50–51 B. Borrell Casals/Frank Lane Picture Agency/Corbis; p. 50 Science Photo Library; p. 51 Naashon Zalk/Corbis.

Cover photograph of a horsefly reproduced with permission of the RSPCA Photolibrary.

The publishers would like to thank Jon Pearce for his assistance in the preparation of this book.

Every effort has been made to contact copyright holders of any material reproduced in this book. Any omissions will be rectified in subsequent printings if notice is given to the publishers.

Disclaimer
All the Internet addresses (URLs) given in this book were valid at the time of going to press. However, due to the dynamic nature of the Internet, some addresses may have changed, or sites may have changed or ceased to exist since publication. While the author and publishers regret any inconvenience this may cause readers, no responsibility for any such changes can be accepted by either the author or the publishers.

The paper used to print this book comes from sustainable resources.

Contents

Some words are shown in **bold.** You can find out what they mean by looking in the glossary. You can also look out for them in the "Wild Words" bank at the bottom of each page.

Incredible Insects

Would you believe it?

- Many insects are so small you cannot see them. Some fairy flies are just 0.008 in. (0.2 mm) long.

- Yet the giant agrippa moth can have a **wingspan** of 11.8 in. (30 cm).

- The heaviest insect is the Goliath beetle (below) from Africa. It is as heavy as two hen's eggs 3.5 oz (100 g).

Ninety percent of all animals on Earth are insects. Our world is covered with these tiny **arthropods.** All arthropods have their skeletons on the outside of their bodies, like a shell.

Insects are everywhere, apart from in the oceans. Some live in deserts at over 100 °F (40 °C), while some insect eggs can **survive** freezing. Insects have lived on our planet for 400 million years.

We know of about one million different species of insect. But there could be ten times that number.

So, what are insects?

Insects are air-breathing **invertebrates,** although some young take up **oxygen** from water. Each adult has three parts to its body:
- the head and **antennae,** also called feelers;
- the **thorax,** with three pairs of legs and often two pairs of wings;
- the **abdomen,** with the heart and lungs inside.

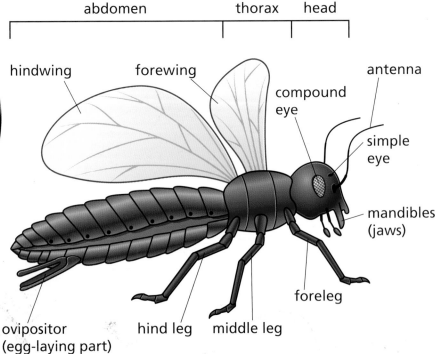

abdomen — thorax — head

hindwing · forewing · compound eye · antenna · simple eye · mandibles (jaws) · foreleg · middle leg · hind leg · ovipositor (egg-laying part)

Wild Words   abdomen   part of the body containing the stomach
arthropod   animal with jointed legs but no backbone

Many types

Some people think that any creepy crawler is an insect. That is not true. Spiders have eight legs and are called **arachnids.** Wood lice have fourteen legs and are called **crustaceans.** Centipedes and millipedes have lots of legs! They are called myriapods.

It can be useful to put the main types of insects into eight groups. There are many other types of insects, too, but this list helps you to see the variety.

Description	Number of species	Examples
Hard wings	400,000	beetles, ladybugs, fireflies, weevils
Scaly wings	150,000	butterflies and moths
Membrane wings	130,000	ants, bees, wasps, termites
Flies	120,000	flies, midges, mosquitoes
Bugs	88,000	aphids, water bugs, cockroaches, earwigs
"Fliers"	36,000	dragonflies, mayflies, damselflies, thrips
"Hoppers"	25,000	crickets, locusts (shown below), stick insects
Bristletails	370	silverfish

Find out later . . .

How do some insects attack others?

How do some insects avoid getting eaten?

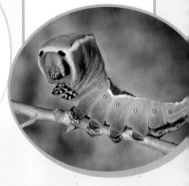

Which insects do we need to fear?

invertebrate   animal without a backbone
thorax   part of the body between the head and abdomen, like a human's chest

Meet the Family

How do all the the groups of insects differ from each other?

Incredible beetles

- The longest living insect is the jewel beetle. The **larvae** can live in trees for more than 35 years before becoming adults. The adults have a far shorter life span.

- Did you know you might have eaten beetles? A female Mexican beetle is crushed to make a red dye and food coloring called cochineal. It is sometimes used in lipstick or in pink icing for cakes.

▶ These cochineal beetles live on a cactus.

Hard wings

A quarter of all animals on the planet are beetles. For every person, there are about 25 million beetles. Some are too small to see, while others are as big as your fist. They all have biting mouth parts and two pairs of wings. The front wings are really just hard wing covers that are not used for flying.

Of the 360,000 different species of beetle, the ladybug is perhaps most people's favorite. It may be because of its color and dots. But gardeners like ladybugs because they eat greenfly, which would otherwise damage plants.

Other beetles are not so popular. About 40,000 species are weevils. These insects have long snouts like a trunk and they can destroy cotton crops, food, and plants.

antennae   insect's feelers
larvae   young of an animal that is very different from the adult

Scaly wings

Butterflies and moths belong to the second-largest family of insects. They have large wings that are scaly and powdery. These **species** go through an amazing change when they mature from the caterpillar stage to the adult.

What is the difference between a butterfly and a moth? Most moths fly at night, while butterflies fly during the day. However, some moths break the rules and fly in daylight, like the clearwing moth. Some people think butterflies are brightly colored and moths are duller. This is not always the case. There are dull butterflies and there are brightly colored moths.

The best way to tell the difference is to look at their **antennae.** Butterflies generally have antennae with small lumps on the end, but moths do not.

Bright butterflies

Many new species of beetles and moths are found each year. There are about six times as many species of moths as there are species of butterflies. Butterflies and many moths have brightly colored scales on their wings. The purpose of these patterns is to attract a mate.

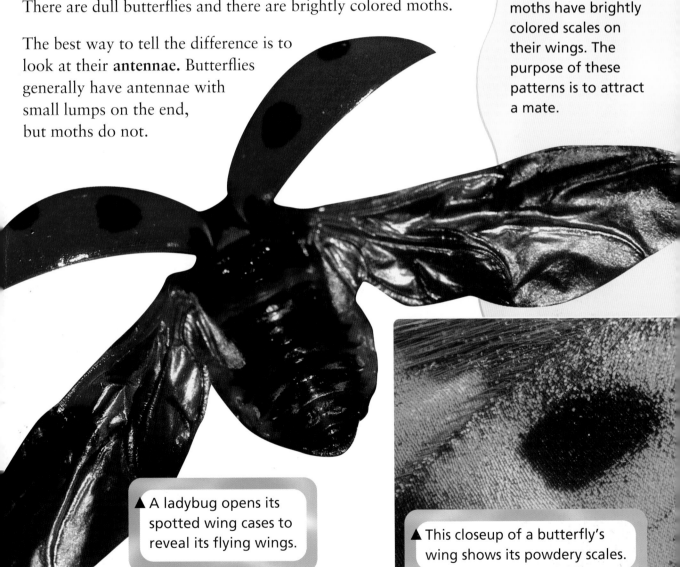

▲ A ladybug opens its spotted wing cases to reveal its flying wings.

▲ This closeup of a butterfly's wing shows its powdery scales.

species   type of animal or plant

Termites

Termites are often called white ants because many are white. They live in large underground nests just like ants. Some nests have tall "chimneys" above ground, like the one below. There are about 2,250 different **species** of termite.

Ants, bees, and wasps

Some insects always seem busy. They live in large groups and have to work hard to keep their nests clean, their young looked after, and their queen fed.

Ants live in **colonies** made up of several classes. These include the winged ants, soldiers, and workers. Workers often carry things. An ant can lift 50 times its own weight. But that is nothing compared to the honeybee, which can lift 300 times its own weight. That is like a person lifting a bus!

All bees, wasps, and ants have a special skill. They can return to their nest after traveling long distances. They seem to have built-in **navigation.** When they find food, they have ways to tell the others where the food is located.

colony   group of individuals living together
navigation   figuring out the right way to get somewhere

Busy bees

Most bumblebees live on their own in burrows or in tree stumps. Some live as far north as the Arctic. Bees are different from wasps because they feed their **larvae** with honey. They make this by collecting **nectar** from plants. Wasps feed their larvae with meat, usually insects that they **paralyze** with their stings.

Good workers

Bees have been important to us for centuries. They produce honey and wax and they help to **pollinate** plants. They do a huge amount of useful work every year.

Ants and wasps help to keep down the numbers of many pests on our crops. They eat caterpillars that harm cereals, vegetables, and fruit. Scientists believe that if these families of insects were to disappear from Earth, our way of life would fall apart.

Overcrowded

The largest recorded colony of insects was a group of ants in Japan. There were more than 300 million ants living in one super-colony of 45 joined nests.

▼ These wood ants are coming out of their nest in the spring.

◄ Honeybee workers store **pollen** and honey in their nest.

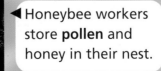

paralyze   stun a creature so it is unable to move
pollinate   transfer pollen to the female parts of a flower to make seeds

Mosquito

The average mosquito has 47 teeth, but it is the mosquito's sharp **proboscis** that causes the trouble. It stabs through our skin to drink blood, which will make us itch.

The female *Anopheles* mosquito can pass a deadly **parasite** into the bloodstream. This spreads the disease malaria. Malaria kills millions of people every year. This makes mosquitoes the deadliest insect known to humans.

▶ A mosquito bites through human skin.

Flies

Flies are all over the world—billions of them. They have troubled us for hundreds of years. The common housefly has followed humankind to every corner of Earth. As it buzzes around a kitchen, a housefly settles on any food it can find. It may have just fed on a rotting rat or on animal droppings. Then it crawls over your pizza. Or it may lay eggs on food we leave uncovered. Maybe that is why we hate flies so much.

The mouth parts of flies can only suck; they cannot chew. They suck up liquids and spit them out again. This spreads disease.

FAST FACTS

- Not all flies can fly. Some fungus gnats, for instance, have given up their wings.
- A housefly always hums in the musical key of F.

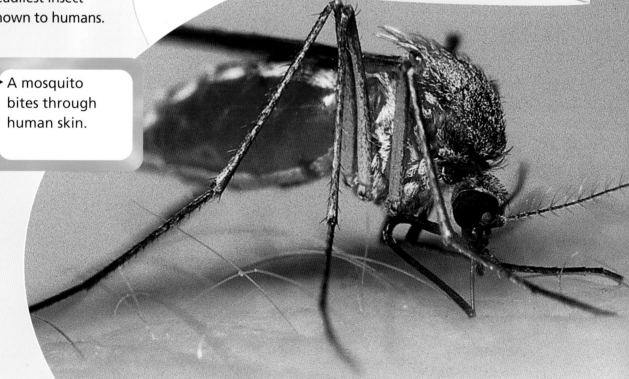

extinct   died out, never to return
parasite   animal or plant that lives in or on another living thing

Bugs

We often call any insect a "bug," but a true bug is an insect with a beaklike mouth for piercing and sucking. There are about 11,000 **species** of bug in North America; 5,600 in Australia; and 1,600 in the United Kingdom. They vary in length from just 0.04 in. (1 mm) to 4.3 in. (11 cm). The largest bugs include earwigs and cockroaches.

The longest of the 1,200 species of earwig is from the island of St. Helena in the South Atlantic. It can reach 3.2 in. (8 cm), but it is now feared to be **extinct.** All earwigs have a narrow body, a pair of **pincers,** and a clawlike tail.

There are nearly 4,000 species of cockroach in the world, but fewer than one percent of them are pests.

Cockroach facts

- The largest known cockroach in the world has a **wingspan** of up to 7.1 in. (18 cm).

- The smallest known cockroach is about 0.2 in. (4 mm) long and lives in the nests of leaf-cutter ants in North America.

- Australian burrowing cockroaches, like those shown above, can weigh the same as a hen's egg.

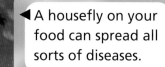
◄ A housefly on your food can spread all sorts of diseases.

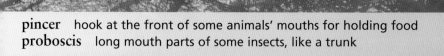
pincer   hook at the front of some animals' mouths for holding food
proboscis   long mouth parts of some insects, like a trunk

"Fliers"

Whether they run, hop, or fly, adult insects know how to move fast. They have to escape from hungry mouths. Those that fly come in many shapes and sizes.

One of the largest is the dragonfly. **Fossils** have been found of dragonflies with **wingspans** of 29.5 in. (75 cm) from 350 million years ago.

Today, dragonflies are fairly common near water in warmer parts of the world. There are about 5,300 **species** worldwide, and these can be divided into two main types. The first type are true dragonflies that rest with their wings out from their bodies in a cross shape. There are also damselflies, which hold their wings parallel to their bodies.

Locusts

Sometimes desert locusts **swarm.** This is when up to 500,000 million locusts meet up. There could be 1.1 million tons of locusts flying in the sky, like a huge thundercloud stretching as far as the eye can see. They eat any plants they find. Such a swarm can eat 22,000 tons of grain in one day. That is enough to feed 20 million people!

▼ Many dragonflies, like this hawker, have bright, sparkling colors.

fossil   very old remains of things that once lived, found in mud and rock

Springtails

Springtails are tiny insects about 0.04 in. (1 mm) long. (The ones on the left here are magnified.) They do the soil good by breaking down dead plant matter. Some are pests to crops. There are more than 6,000 species around the world. Scientists have found there can be 100 million springtails per 11 square feet (1 sq. meter) in the ordinary farm soil of Iowa.

"Hoppers"

Fleas are hoppers and do not fly. They can jump 150 times their body length and 80 times their own height. Most are very small, but the biggest flea in the world, which lives in North America, is about 0.5 in. (12 mm) long.

Grasshoppers have shorter **antennae** than crickets. They rub their back legs to "sing," while crickets rub their front wings. Like locusts and grasshoppers, they hop and fly.

Slow movers

A praying mantis stands still with its front legs together as if it is praying. Stick insects do not need to move quickly, since they are trying to look like twigs. But when a tasty insect comes by, stick insects move fast to grab it. Stick and leaf insects live in the **tropics.**

FAST FACTS

- Thrips are about 0.2 in. (5 mm) long. Swarms of these tiny flies often appear shortly before thunderstorms, so they are also known as thunder flies or thunder bugs.
- The longest stick insect can grow to be over 14 in. (36 cm) long—longer than this book.

swarm   move together in a large group
tropics   parts of the world where it is warm year-round

Amazing Bodies

Walking on water

Pond skaters like the one below can walk on water because they are so light. The **surface tension** on water stops them from sinking. Many waterproof hairs on their legs keep them afloat. They seem to skate over pond water with no trouble at all.

If they do not keep on the move, insects are likely to be eaten by **predators.** Their legs are important for running away from danger. But insect legs work in many different ways.

Legs

Cockroaches have three pairs of strong legs for running very fast. Grasshoppers use their back pair of stronger legs for jumping quickly.

Praying mantises use their front pair of legs like a weapon to catch **prey.** Dragonflies do not use their legs to walk, but rather to catch other insects and hold them up to their mouths.

Butterflies use their legs to taste food, since they have taste buds in them. Other insects use their legs for digging and swimming. Hairy legs are a great help to swimming insects. The hairs trap air and stop them from sinking.

FAST FACTS

Some caterpillars move along in a rippling, up-and-down motion. Others hold the ground with their front legs and pull their body into a loop like this: Ω

predator   animal that hunts and eats other animals
prey   animal that is killed and eaten by other animals

Hopping legs

Fleas are famous for their power-packed legs, which give them a huge flick into the air. With a strong breeze, they can travel a long way. From a sitting position, a flea can easily hop a distance of 11.8 in. (30 cm). That is like a person doing a long jump of 459 ft (140 m). A flea was once recorded jumping over 3 ft (1 m) high. That is like a person hopping over the Empire State Building!

Running legs

Silverfish are small wingless insects that spend most of their life under stones or floorboards. They are extremely fast: the only time you might see one is if it gets trapped in the bathtub. They can wiggle in and out of tiny spaces, such as between the pages of a closed book.

▶ This is a **time-lapse photograph** of a flea jumping.

Human head lice

Some insects do not move if they do not want to. Human head lice cling onto hair with a claw, and they are impossible to remove even when hair is washed and combed. Even using conditioner that makes hair smooth and slippery cannot remove lice. You can only get rid of them by using a special shampoo—or having your head shaved.

▲ This magnified view of a head louse shows it clinging to a hair.

surface tension   fine film across flat, calm liquid that can hold up light objects
time-lapse photograph   photo that shows the stages of an action that happens quickly

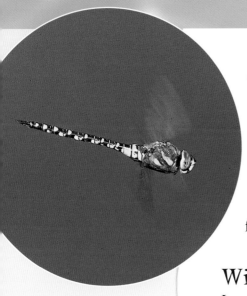

As light as air

Many insects are so light that they can drift around in the air without much effort. Thrips and aphids are so small they can be blown by the wind for long distances. Other light insects can land and walk on ceilings. Sticky pads on their feet keep them from falling. Also, **gravity** has little effect when something is so light. Even if an insect falls, it will not get hurt when it drops on the ground.

Wings

Insect wings are full of tiny veins filled with blood. Butterfly wings are often covered in very small hairs. These trap air and help them flutter. Brightly colored wings allow males and females to recognize each other.

Fast fliers

Dragonflies like the one above are some of the fastest insect fliers. They can fly in bursts of more than 30 mi (48 km) per hour. They often attack other insects in midair. Some migrate long distances.

Hawk moths are thought to be one of the fastest insects. They have been measured flying at 33.3 mi (53.6 km) per hour.

▶ These **time-lapse photographs** show a fly taking off.

gravity   force that pulls all objects toward Earth
migrate   travel in search of food or to breed

- Ladybugs were sent into space in 1999. Even in zero gravity, the ladybugs could fly well and hunt aphids.

- A hover fly is great at flying. One minute it can dart so fast that it is just a blur, and then it can hover and seem to hang in the air, like the one below.

Flying

Most insects have two pairs of wings, but some are wingless, such as lice, fleas, and silverfish. Many flies only have one pair of wings. Most bugs and beetles do not use their front wings for flying, but rather to protect their bodies and flying wings.

A lot of insects are great pilots. They can perform amazing stunts, from landing upside down on a ceiling to hovering over a flower. Butterflies and moths can flutter gently as well as do **vertical** takeoffs and fly backward. Some fly incredible distances. North American monarch butterflies travel more than 1,500 mi (2,400 km) south to Mexico every winter. Other **species migrate** even further and cross the Arctic Circle. The flying skills of many insects are truly amazing.

vertical   going straight up in the air

Seeing colors

For many insects, flowers are food. While feeding, bees and butterflies collect **pollen** grains and transfer them as they feed on other flowers. This **fertilizes** the flowers so that they can produce seeds. To help insects see them, many flowers have striking colors with bright markings. These attract and guide the insects.

Heads and senses

The insect brain may be tiny, but it has a lot to do. It is the control center that must respond to all the signals picked up by the insect's senses. Each insect needs to know where three things are: danger, food, and a mate.

Eyes

Most insects have two **compound** eyes, which are made up of any number of single eyes. They help the insect to see moving objects clearly and to figure out distances. Dragonflies, with their flying skills, need good eyesight, so their compound eyes are bigger than most other insects' eyes. Simple eyes just tell an insect where it is light or dark. Insects that live under ground or in darkness may have no eyes at all.

▼ Bright colors are a big draw for a bee.

compound   made up of many parts
fertilize   when sperm joins an egg to form a new individual

Signals

Insects use sounds to help them make sense of their surroundings. They also pick up **vibrations** with their **antennae.**

Grasshoppers and locusts have ears on their **abdomen.** These help pick up sounds of their own **species** so that they do not become separated. The lacewing picks up sound vibrations with its wings, while ants do so with their legs.

Crickets spend a lot of time chirping to each other. But their ears might not be where you would expect them to be. Crickets have their ears in their front legs.

Hairy legs are important for cockroaches, too. Tiny bristles sense sound vibrations and warn them if a heavy foot is about to stomp.

Night flight

Lights often attract insects at night. This can be harmful to them if they are attracted to a flame. Experts think one reason why moths fly into a light is because they depend on stars and the moon to find their way. Artificial light upsets their **navigation.**

◀ The compound eyes of an emperor dragonfly are seen clearly here.

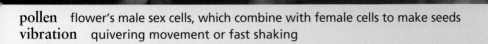

pollen   flower's male sex cells, which combine with female cells to make seeds
vibration   quivering movement or fast shaking

> ▶ A male gypsy moth has an amazing sense of smell.

Finding the right place

Lice use their antennae to sense the warm, damp parts of our bodies that provide a good feed. Hair lice are not too fussy about what sort of hair they choose. Still, they often like to lay their eggs in clean hair.

> ▼ Under the microscope, this head louse on a hair looks like an alien monster.

Antennae

Antennae poke out from an insect's head like two television receptors that pick up signals in the air. They are often called feelers because they are used to touch and feel **vibrations.**

Antennae can often also sense chemical changes around them. Most insects communicate using smell, but they do not have noses. Instead, they have small **sensors** over their bodies, but especially on their antennae.

Many moths have antennae that look like small feathers. These can sense other moths over long distances. A male gypsy moth can smell a female more than 1 mi (1.6 km) away.

A cockroach uses its long antennae to feel its way in the dark. That is how it tracks down crumbs at night as it scurries around the kitchen.

     segment   section or separate part

Picking up signals

Antennae come in a wide range of shapes, sizes, and lengths. Each antenna is divided into **segments.** Scientists can sometimes tell from these segments if two insect **species** are closely related.

Insects that live together in close groups often stroke and groom each other with their antennae. Honeybees use theirs to communicate messages.

A bee will sometimes fly into the hive and dance. It waggles its **abdomen** and moves in a figure eight. The other bees crowd around and touch the dancing bee with their antennae. This tells the other bees which direction to fly and how far away any flowers are located.

Heat sensors

Blood-sucking insects use their antennae to sense the heat from **warm-blooded** animals. Mosquitoes and botflies can feel temperature changes and then fly in for a drink of blood. For some reason, it seems that mosquitoes are particularly attracted to people who have just eaten bananas!

▼ A mosquito's feathery antennae can be seen in this magnified photograph.

sensor device that picks up signals
warm-blooded able to keep the body warm even if the outside temperature is cold

Finding air

- Mosquito **larvae** hatch in water, but they have to get oxygen from the air. They breathe through tiny tubes that they poke out of the water.

- Diving beetles like the one below collect bubbles of air at the surface and carry these bubbles underwater with them as a source of oxygen.

Breathing

All animals need to take **oxygen** into their bodies. Their blood takes the oxygen to the muscles, organs, and brain. These let out **carbon dioxide,** which the body needs to get rid of. Land animals do this by breathing with lungs, while fish breathe with **gills.** The gills are slits near the head, which take oxygen from water flowing through them.

Most insects breathe through tiny tubes inside their body called **tracheae.** Air enters the tubes through holes in the sides of the body. Insects such as water beetles and water boatmen still breathe like this. They regularly have to rise to the surface to take in fresh air. However, their **larvae** do not have to worry—they are born with gills.

> > > > > > > > > > >
Find out more about larvae on page 34.

carbon dioxide   gas that animals breathe out
oxygen   one of the gases in air and water that all living things need

Strange bodies

The larvae of dragonflies, damselflies, stoneflies, and mayflies breathe through gills. They hatch in water, where some grow and develop for up to five years before they climb out. Then they shed their skin and fly off as adults that breathe through tracheae.

Insect blood is rich in **nutrients,** but not as rich in oxygen as our blood. It is not red, either, but usually a watery green. The insect heart is a tube that runs along its back. It beats to swish the blood around the body. This keeps the important oxygen flowing to all the organs and muscles.

Insect blood does not flow through blood vessels as ours does. It flows through spaces inside the insect's body.

▲ An elephant cannot get rid of its lice by taking a shower.

Breathing under water

Even though lice do not have gills, they will not drown if their **host** goes swimming. Tiny air bubbles trapped in skin **pores** or hair will give lice enough oxygen to **survive.**

◄ Water boatmen row themselves through the water by using their hairy legs as oars.

pores   tiny holes in the skin
tracheae   tubes through which air passes

Feeding

Tear moths

A moth from Southeast Asia gets a drink in the strangest way. It feeds on the water in the eyes of cows. It settles under their eyes and drinks their tears. These tear moths do not seem to upset the cows.

The mouths of insects vary according to what they eat. Some, like hawk moths, have tongues up to 5.9 in. (15 cm) long. These are for going deep into flowers to find **nectar.** The male mosquito also feeds on plant juices. But the female mosquito's **proboscis** has a needle point to break skin and drink blood.

Some ants can bite through tough skin, including a human's. Their jaws are strong, so they can grip and cut up other insects.

Flies can only suck liquids. When a fly lands on solid food, it spits juices onto it from its spongy mouth pad. This **dissolves** the food into a soupy mess, which the fly can then suck up.

► The jaws of a leaf-cutter ant are like saws.

crop   pouch in the throat for storing food
dissolve   break down into a liquid

Digestion

Once food gets into an insect's mouth, it begins to break down. **Saliva** and other juices along the digestive system work on the food so that it is ready to go through the **abdomen.** Here, the food is absorbed into the insect's blood. The **nutrients** are then taken to the body.

Many insects have a **crop** below their mouths. This is a storage pouch that lets the insect gulp down food quickly. The crop can then empty over time as the food passes into a **gizzard.** This is very useful for animals that do not have teeth in their mouths. The gizzard is like a second mouth that grinds up solid bits of food before they pass into the stomach. Any waste passes through the insect and is finally pushed out.

Thirsty beetle

Even in dry deserts, some beetles manage to get moisture. The darkling beetle of Africa's Namib Desert (shown below) points its abdomen into the sea mist. Tiny droplets of water collect on its body, which it then licks.

gizzard extra stomach that grinds down food
saliva juices made in the mouth to help chewing and digestion

Jumping beans

Caterpillars from a Mexican moth hatch inside a bean that grows on a plant. They feed on the seeds inside the bean (shown below). When the bean falls to the ground, the caterpillar inside moves around suddenly. This makes the bean hop around. Children in Mexico hold races with these "jumping beans."

Plant-eaters

Over half of all insect species are **herbivores.** That means they only eat plants or parts of plants. These might be leaves, stalks, roots, **pollen, nectar,** seeds, fruit, bark, or wood. Any gardener will know of the many insects or **larvae** that can infest and destroy plants. Farmers spend a fortune on **insecticides** to stop their crops from being ruined. Not all attacks are as dramatic as locust **swarms** that can strip a field in minutes. Most tiny insects are unseen as they chew, suck, or drill into plants. It is our fault there are so many insects in the world. Farming on such a large scale has let insect numbers grow. Without humans providing so much food, there would be fewer insects in the world.

FAST FACTS

Millions of insects are eaten by wild animals such as fish and birds every day. If these animals disappear, insect numbers will grow out of control.

fertilizer　substance that allows the soil to feed plants
herbivore　animal that only eats plants; a vegetarian

Insect gardeners

The leaf-cutter ant does not eat leaves, but rather cuts them up for **compost.** It takes them to its nest to feed to a special type of **fungus** that it grows for food. The fungus gardens are deep inside the ants' nest. As leaves reach the nest, they are cut up and licked clean of anything that may harm the growth of the harvest fungus. Next, the ants spread out the leaf bits mixed with their droppings . This acts as **fertilizer.** As the fungus grows, it is fed to the members of the **colony.**

Many termites feed on wood, which is hard to **digest.** The termites have help from tiny animals that live inside their **abdomen.** They are called **protozoa,** and they help the termites break down the wood fibers.

Plants that bite back

Some plants get their revenge on nibbling insects. The Venus fly trap (shown above) waits for a fly to land on it before its leaves snap shut and trap the insect inside. The sundew traps insects on its sticky hairs. These plants slowly digest the captured insects.

◀ These leaf-cutter ants are carrying leaf pieces that they will use to make compost.

insecticide   chemical sprayed to poison insects
protozoa   very tiny living things that can only be seen with a microscope

Scavengers

A number of flies, such as the flesh fly and the bluebottle shown below, lay their eggs in rotting flesh. **Carrion** beetles also go for a dead animal and begin chewing. Such insects are the undertakers of the animal world and help to keep the **environment** clean.

Predators

Many insects kill. One third of all insects are either **predators** or **parasites.** Tiger beetles, wasps, and ants are active hunters. They spend a lot of time looking for **prey.** Other insects wait for prey to come to them. A praying mantis keeps very still. When prey comes close, it thrusts out its legs to catch it. The mantis bites the neck of its prey to **paralyze** it, and then it begins to eat. The mantis almost always starts eating the insect while it is still alive. This makes sure that the insect's struggle is soon over, so it does not attract other predators. A praying mantis eats beetles, butterflies, spiders, crickets, and even small tree frogs, lizards, mice, hummingbirds, or other passing mantises.

▼ A praying mantis waits to strike.

carrion   dead and rotting flesh
environment   natural surroundings

Parasites

Insects need to lay their eggs close to food. **Larvae** must eat when they hatch. To make sure the food is fresh and warm, some flies lay their eggs inside living animals. Their larvae, called maggots, hatch and feed on live meat.

Warble flies lay eggs on cattle, and their larvae burrow into cowhide. They feed inside a cow's flesh until they are ready to fly away.

The sheep nostril fly also lays eggs on a live **host.** The eggs hatch in a sheep's nose and burrow into its eyes and brain. Other flies depend on the host licking eggs and getting them into its stomach. Many horses swallow botfly larvae, which then grow in the horse's **intestines.** Most pass out in the horse's droppings, but some burrow into its blood vessels.

Eaten alive

Some flies lay their eggs on spiders. The larvae hatch and eat their way through the spider's body. Some wasps inject their eggs into caterpillars. The eggs hatch out and slowly eat the caterpillar alive— from the inside.

▼ These wasp larvae have come out of a hawk moth caterpillar to form **cocoons.**

host   animal or plant that has another animal or plant living in or on it

Disgusting meals

Some insects have the most disgusting taste. Their mouths water at the sight of blood, rotting flesh, or dung. The worse the smell, the faster they arrive.

Lice

Sucking lice feed on fresh, warm blood, and they only live on **mammals.** That can include humans. A female louse will lay about 300 eggs at the rate of about 10 eggs a day. The eggs take five to ten days to hatch. The **larvae** will not leave in a hurry, even if the **host** happens to die. Lice can **survive** for up to three days on a dead body. Then they hitch a ride on a passing fly to be taken to a new host.

Blood

Although fleas can live for a few months without food, they cannot survive or lay eggs without blood. Adult fleas that have just come out of their **cocoon** can only live about one week if they cannot get a blood meal. The flea above is feeding on a mouse.

▶ Dung beetles roll a dung ball back home. They are among the strongest insects and can lift 50 times their own weight.

cocoon   silky case that protects larvae
mammal   warm-blooded animal with hair that feeds its young with milk

Dung

Flies like to lay eggs in dung. A cowpat can hatch out 2,000 flies. In Australia there are around 20 million cows dropping twelve cowpats each a day. That means a lot of flies!

Luckily, dung beetles eat dung. They gather fresh dung into balls to roll into underground nests. The female lays an egg into each dung-ball and covers the nest with soil. Without these beetles, the world would be piled with dung.

Cows were only brought into Australia in 1788, so the dung beetles there were only used to kangaroo dung. They would not eat wet, smelly cow dung. Dung beetles from Europe and Africa had to be brought in to deal with the cowpats and cut down on the number of flies.

June 17, 2003
Live beetles appear in boy's urine

A thirteen-year-old boy in India has amazed doctors. Live winged beetles appeared in his urine. He said: "No one believed me when I told them about these flies." A doctor treating him at Bengal hospital said, "This is a very rare condition called myiasis, in which a human or animal body, dead or alive, is invaded by the larvae of particular flies."

◄ Maggots like these were once used in hospitals to clean wounds. They ate dead flesh, which helped the wound to heal.

Breeding

Gift-wrapped

Before they mate, male dance flies give their partners a present of a dead insect wrapped in silk. The female is so busy unwrapping this that the male can mate with her without being eaten. Sometimes he fools her by wrapping up nothing.

An insect's life is usually short. Finding a mate and making more insects become urgent jobs.

Meeting

Insects have many ways of finding and attracting partners. Their **antennae** are tuned in to seek out a partner. The female is often gives off chemicals to help the male find her. Sometimes the male "sings" for her, or he will "dance" using his antennae and wings. As soon as they meet, the insects often rub antennae or legs.

Male fireflies are kind of flashy. They attract a mate by glowing in the dark. The males have light organs under their **abdomens.** The dancing greenish-yellow to reddish-orange lights seem to impress the wingless female. Sometimes, after **mating,** her eggs will even start to glow.

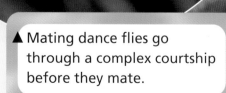

▲ Mating dance flies go through a complex courtship before they mate.

mating   when a male and female animal come together to produce young

Mating

Male insects are often smaller than the females. This can be dangerous if the female is used to eating smaller insects. The male has to transfer **sperm** into her body without being eaten by her. Often the male will throw up to give the female something to eat.

The female stores his sperm inside her body until she releases her eggs to be **fertilized.** She finds somewhere safe with food close by to lay the eggs. Some insects, such as aphids and tsetse flies, give birth to live young. Many water bugs carry their eggs on their backs and look after their young once they have hatched. Female earwigs like to keep things tidy by licking their eggs clean.

▲ This wood wasp is laying her eggs into beetle larvae under the bark.

Wood wasps

The **larvae** of some wasps and beetles grow hidden under tree bark. But a female wood wasp can sense these larvae under the bark. She injects her eggs through the bark and right into a larva. When the wood wasp eggs hatch, the larva feed on and kill their young **hosts**.

◄ A firefly looking for a partner gives off a warm glow!

sperm   male sex cell

Young and parents

Insect eggs hatch into either tiny wriggling **larvae** or into small adults called **nymphs.** The nymphs of dragonflies, cockroaches, and grasshoppers do not have wings, only small wing buds. Most nymphs shed their skin as their bodies get bigger.

The female mayfly lives underwater for up to three years as a nymph. When she becomes an adult and grows her full wings, she has about a day to **mate** and lay her eggs. She cannot eat or drink and will die within the day.

Many young insects go through major changes to become adults. This is called **metamorphosis.** A larva will eat for a few weeks, shed its skin, and then become a **pupa.** Many insects go through these four stages: egg, larva, pupa, and adult.

Strange timing

Cicadas are large bugs that make a chirping sound. There are about 1,500 **species** around the world, and their nymphs live in soil. In North America, some cicada nymphs take seventeen years to shed their skins and become adults. Millions of adults emerge at the same time.

▲ This cicada is magnified several times.

emerge   come out into view
metamorphosis   change from being a larva to being an adult

Young mantids

Female mantids, such as the praying mantis, lay groups of 12 to 400 eggs in a frothy liquid. This hardens into a shell where the tiny insects **survive** during the winter. There are about 1,800 species of mantis, and some even survive winters in the northeastern United States. They were brought there to keep down the populations of other insects.

Tiny mantid nymphs **emerge** in the spring. Their first meal is often one of their brothers or sisters. The nymphs look like ants at first, then they grow during the summer as they eat aphids (greenfly) and flies. Finally, they shed their last skin and emerge as fully grown adults.

▶ Mantid nymphs look like small versions of the adults.

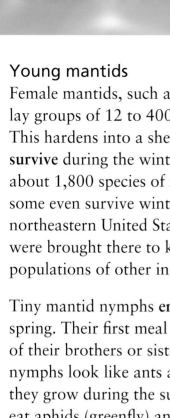

Did you know?

Leafhoppers and froghoppers are small bugs that suck sap from plant stems. As nymphs, they wrap themselves in bubbly froth to protect them from the sun and from **predators**. These bubbles are often called cuckoo spit, shown above.

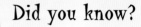

STOP PRESS

A Cambridge University professor has discovered that froghoppers are the kings of the jumping world. They can leap similar distances to fleas, despite being 60 times heavier.

nymph   in-between stage from larva to adult
pupa   stage when a larva is developing into an adult inside a shell or cocoon

Life cycle

It is amazing how a crawling caterpillar can change into a fluttering butterfly or moth. It completely changes in shape and colors—and it suddenly knows how to fly.

The female monarch butterfly lays about 400 eggs under the leaves of milkweed plants. The yellow eggs take about two weeks to hatch. The new caterpillar is only 0.08 in. (2 mm) long, but it eats right away. On the first day of its life, it eats its own weight in food. The tiny caterpillars begin to strip the milkweed leaves as they munch through the plant.

Do not touch

The caterpillars of the monarch butterfly (shown below) are brightly colored and striped. This is a warning to **predators** that they taste horrible and should be left alone. The caterpillars eat milkweed leaves that make them poisonous.

When it reaches 2 in. (5 cm), a caterpillar begins to change into a **pupa.** It weaves a small silk button under a leaf, sticks to it, and waits.

chrysalis   pupa of a butterfly or moth with a hard outer case

New life

Inside its casing, the pupa is slowly changing shape and color. The outer layer hardens into a green case with gold dots. This is known as the **chrysalis,** which is the Greek word for *golden*. Inside, strange things are happening. A butterfly is slowly forming.

When the butterfly starts to **emerge** two weeks later, its wings are droopy and wet. It clings to the old chrysalis case while fluid from its **abdomen** is pumped into the veins of the wings. After a few hours, the wings are dry with no creases. The butterfly is now ready to fly away. All it has to do next is find a mate, and the process starts again.

◀ This monarch butterfly has just emerged from its chrysalis.

On the move

Each fall thousands of monarch butterflies gather in southern Canada before **migrating** south to Mexico. But many of the trees in Mexico that have been homes to these butterflies for years are being cut down. Monarch butterfly numbers are now falling.

Defense

Insects face danger all the time. Running away is one defense, but sometimes other tricks help them **survive**.

A prickly customer

Camouflage is a great defense. Treehopper bugs from Florida look like thorns, as seen below. Even if a predator does risk taking a bite, the treehopper's shape makes it stick in most throats.

Color and camouflage

Looks can be a matter of life and death. An insect will soon be someone's dinner if it is easily seen. Insects that chew leaves all day are easy targets for **predators**. Leaf-eating insects have **evolved** many ways to survive attack. For instance, many **species** feed only at night, when there are fewer birds around. Insects often hide by feeding on the undersides of leaves. Beetles drop off a plant as soon as they sense a predator is near.

camouflage   color or pattern that matches the background
disguise   change of appearance to look different

How to stay safe

Some insects are experts at staying hidden. Moths with **mottled** brown wings can stay safely on tree trunks, and bark bugs look just like tiny bumps on a tree. It is difficult to spot stick insects and leaf insects when they sit on a branch. Many insects have just the right coloring to blend into their backgrounds, so they stay unseen.

Disguise is always a good trick. A flower mantis looks like a flower when it sits on a bush. Some grasshoppers stay very still in mud or on rocks and look just like pebbles.

Keep off

Many moths have two large spots on their wings, which look like staring eyes on a scary face. The swallowtail caterpillar (shown above) has a good trick. It has two large eyespots on its back, so it looks like a poisonous snake.

◄ The pupa of a swallowtail butterfly looks like bird droppings, but it turns into a beautiful butterfly.

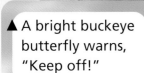

Smart tricks

Leaf-feeding insects have a hard time. They are near the bottom of the **food chain,** and so many other animals want to eat them. These insects have to come up with a few extra tricks to defend themselves. Many do not try to hide at all.

Their bright colors seem to say, "Come and get me." Yet all **predators** know one thing: when an insect is brightly colored, it could mean that it is poisonous. Many colorful insects feed on leaves that make them **toxic.** Their colors simply warn others to keep away. But sometimes harmless insects copy them. Despite being really good to eat, they are covered in bright spots and stripes.

▲ A bright buckeye butterfly warns, "Keep off!"

Colorful tricks

Birds know to leave monarch butterflies alone. The bright orange of the butterfly warns all predators that they are poisonous because of the plants they eat. Even butterflies that are not toxic may copy the monarch butterfly and show bright warning colors.

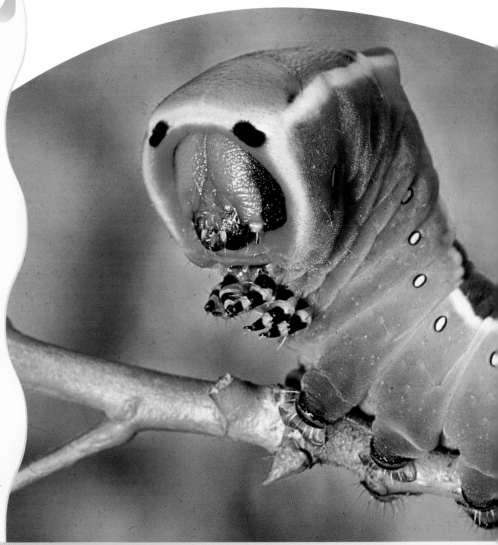

food chain   order in which one living thing feeds on another
gland   part of the body that makes hormones and other substances

Fighting back

One way to scare off attackers is to hit back. Even if a predator is much bigger than you, giving it a shock can give you time to scurry or wriggle away.

The caterpillar of the puss moth puffs up its head if it is under threat. It pokes out a pair of horns, and if that fails, it squirts acid from just under its head. This stings any attacker and makes it think twice.

A wood ant also puts up a fight with a secret weapon. It will lie on its back and poke out its **abdomen,** then squirt acid. It runs off while the attacker's eyes water.

The giant weta is from New Zealand. When under threat, it just kicks out with its strong back legs, which are covered in spines.

Smelly tricks

Another way to avoid being eaten is to smell. The stink bug (shown below) has **glands** near its back legs. When under threat, they ooze a liquid with a disgusting smell. Many stink bugs are brightly colored as an extra warning.

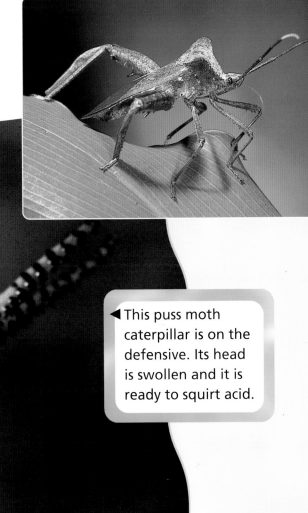

◀ This puss moth caterpillar is on the defensive. Its head is swollen and it is ready to squirt acid.

toxic poisonous

Scary Insects

Some insects have a bad reputation. Many people shiver at the thought of them.

Cockroaches

Everyone seems to hate cockroaches. We think of them swarming in filthy dark places, spreading disease. However, many **species** of cockroach are small and live in very clean places.

Cockroaches are **scavengers,** and they feed on almost anything. Many just eat wood, but a few give all cockroaches a bad name. They spread disease when they go from dirty areas into kitchens. Since they can **contaminate** food, they need to be controlled.

Cockroaches are tough, so it can be difficult to control them. They have been around for millions of years. They can even **survive** doses of **radiation**. Water does not bother them, either. They can survive for 40 minutes without air, so they do not often drown.

Enough to make you shudder

One reason cockroaches are scary is because they can be hard to kill. After all, a cockroach can live for a week without its head. It will only die because it cannot drink water and dries out. A cockroach can survive without food for up to a month.

▼ The giant burrowing cockroach may look scary, but the only thing it is likely to bite is dead leaves in forests in Australia.

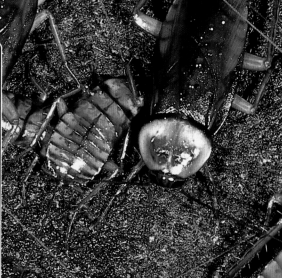

contaminate   spoil and make unsafe
radiation   rays of energy that can be harmful in large amounts

Unwelcome visitors

Most species of cockroach live in the **tropics,** but some can survive at the North and South poles. Yet most cockroaches cannot deal with temperatures much colder than freezing, so they often like to move indoors. They can easily climb walls, since they have claws on their feet. In the days of wooden sailing ships, cockroaches were carried all over the world.

People hate the thought of cockroaches coming from the sewers into their homes. It can be horrible to find them in your kitchen or bathroom as they scurry around at night.

"Ghost cockroaches" like the one below are often seen at night. A cockroach that has just shed its skin is white with black eyes. After about eight hours, the shell returns to its normal color.

◄ There are more than 3,000 species of cockroach. Only 60 species are pests, like these German cockroaches.

On the move

Killer bees first escaped from Brazil in 1957. Swarming killer bees may attack someone 130 ft (40 m) away and chase them for up to 1,310 ft (400 m). Strong smells, bright colors, and loud noises drive them wild. The only advice is to keep running.

FAST FACTS

For a normal, healthy person to get a deadly dose of bee **venom**, it would take about 20 stings for every 2.2 lb (1 kg) of body weight. That is about 1,500 stings at once for a 154-lb (70-kg) person.

▲ These swarming killer bees are in Brazil.

Killer bees

Killer bees sound like insects from a horror movie. But there is a type of bee in Africa that is much more forceful than the normal honeybee. If many of them **swarm** and attack someone, they can be dangerous.

Maybe another bee is scarier. Fifty years ago, Brazilian scientists tried to create a new bee to produce more honey. But they created a bee that turned nasty very quickly. Some escaped and began to spread. They flew north from Brazil and were first seen in the United States in 1990. These new bees will swarm and attack at loud noises. Even jumping into water will not keep them away.

allergy   bad reaction, including sneezing and rashes, to certain substances
venom   poison

Scientists in Texas are working hard to stop the advance of killer bees. They have set traps and are concentrating on queen bees. If they can **fertilize** killer queen bees with **sperm** from ordinary honeybees, they hope to stop more killer bees from hatching.

March 28, 2002

Killer Bees Attack Woman in Las Vegas

A swarm of killer bees attacked a 77-year-old woman in Las Vegas. "She had over 500 stings on her arms, chest, face, and head," a city spokesman said. The woman was in a critical condition at University Medical Center after she was rescued by the fire department.

Dangerous stings

Some people have an **allergy,** which means they can die from bee stings. It is thought that more people die from bee stings each year than from the bites of poisonous snakes. Even so, fewer than one percent of people have a severe reaction to bee stings.

▲ A honeybee's sting and venom sac are at the end of the **abdomen.**

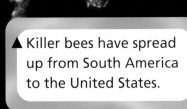
▲ Killer bees have spread up from South America to the United States.

Marching teeth

Army ants kill and eat most animals that do not get out of the way. Together they can kill lizards, snakes, chickens, pigs, goats, scorpions, and many other animals. They also climb trees and eat birds or insects that may live in trees. They have even been known to eat people asleep in their beds.

Scary ants

What animal will eat any other animal in its path, raid ant **colonies,** and march miles to find food? The army ant.

Army ant colonies have one queen and many thousands of workers and soldiers. They travel around together and set up camps. The ants join together to protect the queen and her eggs. They fasten onto each other using their jaws and tiny claws. Their jaws are particularly strong and sharp.

A report told of army ants **swarming** over an area 1 mi (1.6 km) long, moving across Brazil in 1973. It took a real army with flamethrowers to force the ants to march back into the forest.

▶ Army ants swarm over a forest floor in Trinidad.

tissue   soft parts of the body; a collection of cells

Fire ants

Another ant from South America can be scary. Red fire ants inject **venom** that burns and blisters the skin. The venom begins to break down cells and **tissues** and can make someone feel very sick. These ants are now common in parts of the United States.

Red fire ants reached Alabama in the 1930s on cargo ships. Colonies soon began to spread. The first time people knew about them was in 1942. Ed Wilson, a thirteen-year-old boy, came across a mound on the land next to his home. Scientists were amazed to see them, and also to find that each colony had more than one queen. This is seen only with the North American red fire ant. Within 30 years, these ants had swept across the southern United States.

Stinging ants

The bulldog ant of Australia, like the one below, has strong jaws. It bites without letting go and injects strong venom. As few as 30 stings from an ant like this can kill a human.

47

Insects in Danger

Looks can kill

In parts of Europe, the hornet (shown below) is under threat due to its bad image. People kill them because they look harmful, but they rarely attack humans. Now people are trying to protect them in southern England, and their numbers are starting to rise. They have also been introduced to Canada and the United States.

With so many **species** of insects in the world, we are not always aware of those in danger of them being lost forever. Being so small and often out of sight, many insects will not be missed until it is too late. People care less about insects than larger animals because we do not see most of them, and those that we do see are often pests.

For many years we have been at war with insects. We have soaked much of our planet with **insecticides.** We destroy their nests and **habitats.** People catch butterflies, moths, and beetles to display in glass cases. A number of species are now **endangered.**

endangered   at risk of disappearing forever
habitat   natural home of an animal

Three victims

There is an insect that lives in an seven-mile (11-kilometer) stretch of sand dunes in Utah. It has a long name, but it is only 0.4 in. (1 cm) long. It is called the coral pink sand dune tiger beetle. There are about 1,000 left. Collectors take them because of their shiny colors and stunning appearance. Off-road vehicles also disturb their habitat.

The American burying beetle has orange and black stripes. It is the largest **carrion** beetle in North America. This beetle is on the endangered list because there are fewer animals for it to eat. Boston University has released some of these beetles into the wild in Massachusetts.

The basking malachite is a shiny green damselfly about 1.8 in. (4.5 cm) long. There are now only about 1,000 left in South Africa, since cattle have destroyed the riverbanks where they breed.

Making a comeback

Although it is called the large blue butterfly, it only has a **wingspan** of 0.8 in. (2 cm). Clearing hillsides for farming and the use of weed killers and insecticides wiped out this butterfly from Great Britain in 1979. It was reintroduced in 1983, and since then a small number have bred in the wild.

◀ This burying beetle is feeding on the body of a dead animal.

Insects help police

A dead body soon starts to rot. Insects eat it or lay their eggs inside the **tissues**. Scientists have found that different insects arrive in a particular order. This can help them figure out the time of death of a murder victim.

Insects and us

We often think of insects as things to be crushed rather than as animals of value. Yet without insects, our planet would starve.

Many insects are very useful to us. They help keep Earth clean, they help plants make fruit seeds, and they feed millions of animals.

Yet we still shiver at the thought of fleas, lice, and cockroaches in our homes. Termites eat wood and cause great damage to houses. Pests such as the Colorado beetle attack potato crops in many parts of the world and cause great suffering. Locusts wipe out crops and cause **famine**.

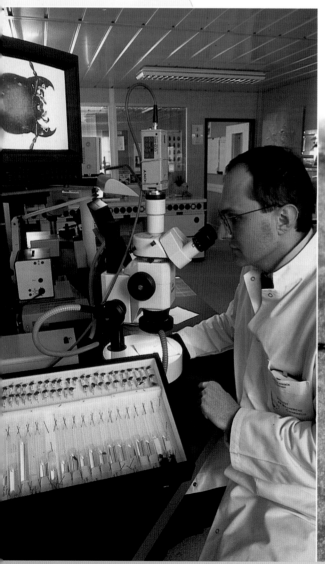

▼ Colorado beetles like these can destroy tomato and pepper plants as well as potatoes.

　famine　long period of poor crops, no harvest, and no food

Curse and blessing

We are never far from insects. Most of the time, we are unaware of them—until they bite or sting us or spread disease to our animals or to us. In 1350, fleas on black rats spread a disease called bubonic plague, killing one-third of all Europeans.

Yet the insect world is finely balanced. If we use poisons to destroy one insect pest, this will have an impact on many other **species**. Many insects are a great help to the soil and to plants. Insects are vital to the world's **food chains**. Insects keep our planet alive.

FAST FACTS

A bat can eat as many as 600 mosquito-sized insects in one hour. An average-sized bat **colony** may eat 500,000 insects in one night.

A deadly curse

The *Anopheles* mosquito is the most deadly animal on the planet. It carries the disease malaria, which in the last 2,000 years may have caused half of all human deaths. It still kills between two million and four million people each year.

Bill Gates, the world's richest man (shown above), has given $168 million to help scientists find a cure for this deadly disease.

Find Out More

Websites

Bugbios
The "Entophiles" pages have great photos of insects.
insects.org

Smithsonian Institute National Zoological Park
Website with articles, information, and many photos of all kinds of animals.
nationalzoo.si.edu

Books

Legg, Gerald. *The World of Insect Life*. Milwaukee: Gareth Stevens, 2002.

Solway, Andrew. *Classfying Insects*. Chicago: Heinemann Library, 2003.

Spilsbury, Louise, and Richard Spilsbury. *Animal Groups: Life in a Colony of Ants*. Chicago: Heinemann Library, 2003.

World Wide Web

If you want to find out more about insects, you can search the Internet using keywords such as this:

- "insect flight"
- swallowtail + caterpillar
- stick insect

You can also find your own keywords by using headings or words from this book. Use the following search tips to help you find the most useful websites.

Search tips

There are billions of pages on the Internet, so it can be difficult to find exactly what you want to find. For example, if you just type in "water" on a search engine such as Google, you will get a list of millions webpages! These search skills will help you find useful websites more quickly:

- Use simple keywords instead of whole sentences.
- Use two to six keywords in a search, putting the most important words first.
- Be precise—only use names of people, places, or things.
- If you want to find words that go together, put quote marks around them.
- Use the advanced section of your search engine.
- Use the "+" sign between keywords to link them.

Where to search

Search engine

A search engine looks through millions of websites and lists all sites that match the words in the search box. It can give thousands of links, but the best matches are at the top of the list, on the first page. Try google.com.

Search directory

A search directory is like a library of websites that have been sorted by a person instead of a computer. You can search by keyword or subject and browse through the different sites like you look through books on a library shelf. A good example is yahooligans.com.

Numbers of incredible creatures

Creatures (y-axis): Amphibians, Mammals, Reptiles, Birds, Fish, Arachnids, Mollusks, Insects

Number of species (approximate): 0, 20,000, 40,000, 60,000, 80,000, 100,000, 120,000, 140,000, 160,000, 180,000, 1,000,000

Glossary

abdomen   part of the body containing the stomach

aggressive   hostile, angry, and bad-tempered

allergy   bad reaction, including sneezing and rashes, to certain substances

antenna (more than one: antennae)   insect's feeler

arachnid   arthropods with eight legs, including spiders and scorpions

arthropod   animal with jointed legs but no backbone

camouflage   color or pattern that matches the background

carbon dioxide   gas that animals breathe out

carrion   dead and rotting flesh

chrysalis ("kris-a-lis")   pupa of a butterfly or moth, with a hard outer case

cocoon   silky case that protects larvae

colony   group of individuals living together

compost   manure or rotting plants used to enrich the soil

compound   made up of many parts

contaminate   spoil and make unsafe

crop   pouch in the throat for storing food

crustacean ("krust-ay-shun")   sea animals with a hard shell, including crabs, lobsters, and shrimp

digest   break down food in the body

disguise   change of appearance to look different

dissolve   break down into a liquid

emerge   come out into view

endangered   at risk of disappearing forever

environment   natural surroundings

evolve   develop and change over time

extinct   died out, never to return

famine   long period of poor crops, no harvest, and no food

fertilize   when sperm joins an egg to form a new individual

fertilizer   substances that allow the soil to feed plants

food chain   order in which one living thing feeds on another

fossil   very old remains of things that once lived, found in mud and rock

fungus   type of mold that grows in damp places

gills   organs that some animals have to breathe underwater

gizzard   extra stomach that grinds down food

gland   part of the body that makes hormones and other substances

gravity   force that pulls all objects toward Earth

habitat   natural home of an animal

herbivore   animal that has only eats plants; a vegetarian

host   animal or plant that has another animal or plant living in or on it

insecticide   chemical sprayed to poison insects

intestines   end part of the digestive system after the stomach

invertebrate   animal without a backbone

larva (more than one: larvae)   young of an animal that is very different from the adult

mammal   warm-blooded animal with hair that feeds its young with milk

mating   when a male and female animal come together to produce young

metamorphosis   change from being a larva to being an adult

migrate   travel in search of food or to breed

navigation   figuring out the right way to get somewhere

nectar   sugary liquid made by plants

nutrient   important substance found in food and needed by the body

nymph   in-between stage from larva to adult

oxygen   one of the gases in air and water that all living things need

paralyze   stun a creature so it is unable to move

parasite   animal or plant that lives in or on another living thing

pincer   hook at the front of some animals' mouths for holding food

pollen   flower's male sex cells, which combine with female cells to make seeds

pollinate   transfer pollen to the female parts of a flower to make seeds

pores   tiny holes in the skin

predator   animal that hunts and eats other animals

prey   animal that is killed and eaten by other animals

proboscis   long mouth parts of some insects, like a trunk

protozoa   very tiny living things that can only be seen with a microscope

pupa   stage when a larva is developing into an adult inside a shell or cocoon

radiation   rays of energy that can be harmful in large amounts

saliva   juices made in the mouth to help chewing and digestion

scavenger   animal that feeds off scraps and the food of others

segment   section or separate part

sensor   device that picks up signals

species   type of animal or plant

sperm   male sex cell

surface tension   fine film across flat, calm liquid that can hold up light objects

survive   stay alive despite danger and difficulties

swarm   move together in a large group

thorax   part of the body between the head and abdomen, like a human's chest

time-lapse photograph   photo that shows the stages of an action that happens quickly

tissue   soft parts of the body; a collection of cells

toxic   poisonous

tracheae   tubes through which air passes

tropics   parts of the world where it is warm all year round

venom   poison

vertical   going straight up in the air

vibration   quivering movement or fast shaking

warm-blooded   able to keep the body warm even if the outside temperature is cold

wingspan   distance from one wing tip to the other with both wings fully stretched

Index